Let the Wind Push Us Across

To Anne,
Thank you
for your enthusiastic
support —

ALSO BY JANE SCHAPIRO

Tapping This Stone (poetry)

Inside a Class Action:
The Holocaust and the Swiss Banks (non-fiction)

Mrs. Cave's House (poetry)

Let the Wind Push Us Across

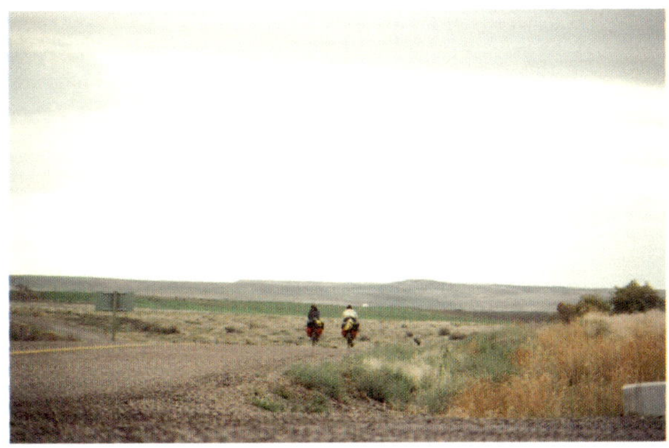

Poems by

Jane Schapiro

with photographs by Shin-ichi Kumanomido

Antrim House

Simsbury, Connecticut

Library of Congress Control Number: 2017931485

ISBN: 978-1-943826-23-0

First Edition, 2017

Printed & bound by Ingram Spark

Book design by Rennie McQuilkin

Photographs by Shin-ichi Kumanomido

Author photograph by Scott Brown

Antrim House
860.217.0023
AntrimHouse@comcast.net
www.AntrimHouseBooks.com
21 Goodrich Road, Simsbury, CT 06070

In memory of our father Ed Schapiro
("Make it to the Atlantic")
&
in celebration of sisters:
Ellen and Barb Schapiro; Naomi, Tamara and Eliana Brown;
Deena Charnofsky and Debbie Fordyce

ACKNOWLEDGMENTS

"Sometimes in the Morning" and its accompanying photo originally appeared untitled in Bourgeononline.com.

Thank you to my mother Nancy Schapiro, who always understood the "why" of our trip and to my first reader and husband, Scott Brown. Special thanks to my daughter Eliana, who insisted that a visual poetic narrative could best capture the spirit of our adventure and breathed life into this project; to my sister Ellen who understands the resonance of those miles so many years after; and to Kuma, whose photos became our lasting treasure.

I am grateful to Robert Rennie McQuilkin of Antrim House and to friend and poet Naomi Thiers for their editorial guidance.

In 1976, my sister Ellen and I dropped out of college to bicycle across the country. Our dream was to dip our back tires in the Pacific and our front tires in the Atlantic. On September 4, 1976, we began our journey. Carrying our packed bikes over the rocky shore of Seaside, Oregon, Ellen and I dipped our rear wheels in the Pacific. Eleven weeks and 3500 miles later we arrived at Crescent Beach, Florida, where we dipped our front wheels in the Atlantic. In between, we crossed the Rockies, pedaled into the Texas Panhandle's cold winds, and faced both the warmth and bigotry of the Deep South. We had no cell phone or Internet, and became fully immersed in the surrounding world. Along the way, people would repeatedly ask us why. Why would two girls take to the road on their bikes? After nearly 40 years, I offer my answer through these poems and photographs. The photographs of our journey were taken by Shin-ichi Kumanomido, a St. Louis architect who quit his job to pursue his own dream of becoming a photographer. He learned about our trip through a mutual friend, and together we merged our dreams.

Jane Schapiro

Table of Contents

I think that what we're seeking is an experience of being alive, so that our life experiences on the purely physical plane will have resonances with our own innermost being and reality, so that we actually feel the rapture of being alive.

– Joseph Campbell

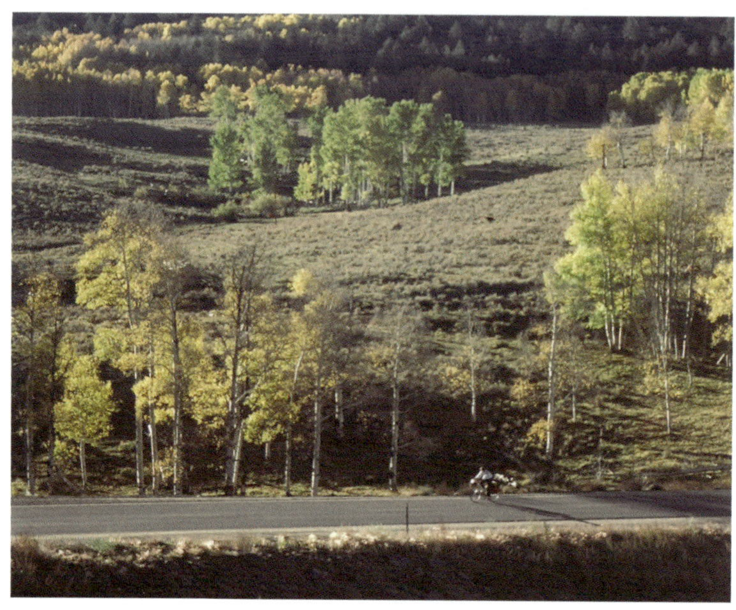

Let the Wind Push Us Across

The Idea

A desk, an open window, first floor Palmer Hall.
Inside: a professor. Outside: a birch.
Inside: a lecture. Outside: a breeze.
Inside: words dry as kindling.
Outside: leaves flickering like sparks.
"Please," I begged my sister,
"we'll pedal west to east,
let the wind push us across."

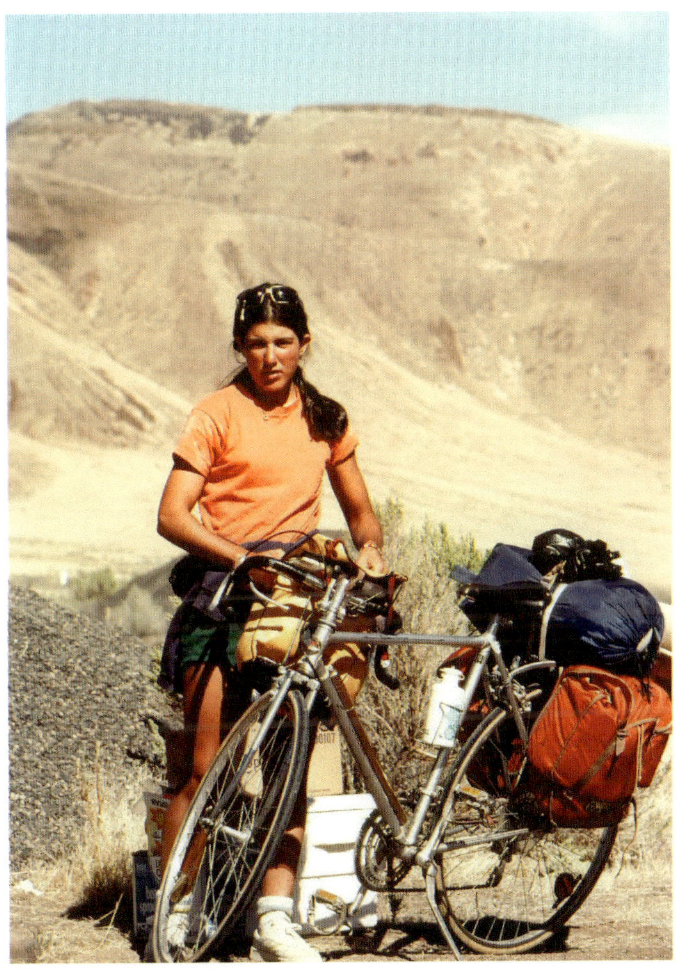

Father

On bikes?
Two girls?
From where?
To where?
How long?
And school?
Career?
On hold?
The nights?
A tent?
The wind?
The cold?
Which roads?
Start when?
Alone?

What for?

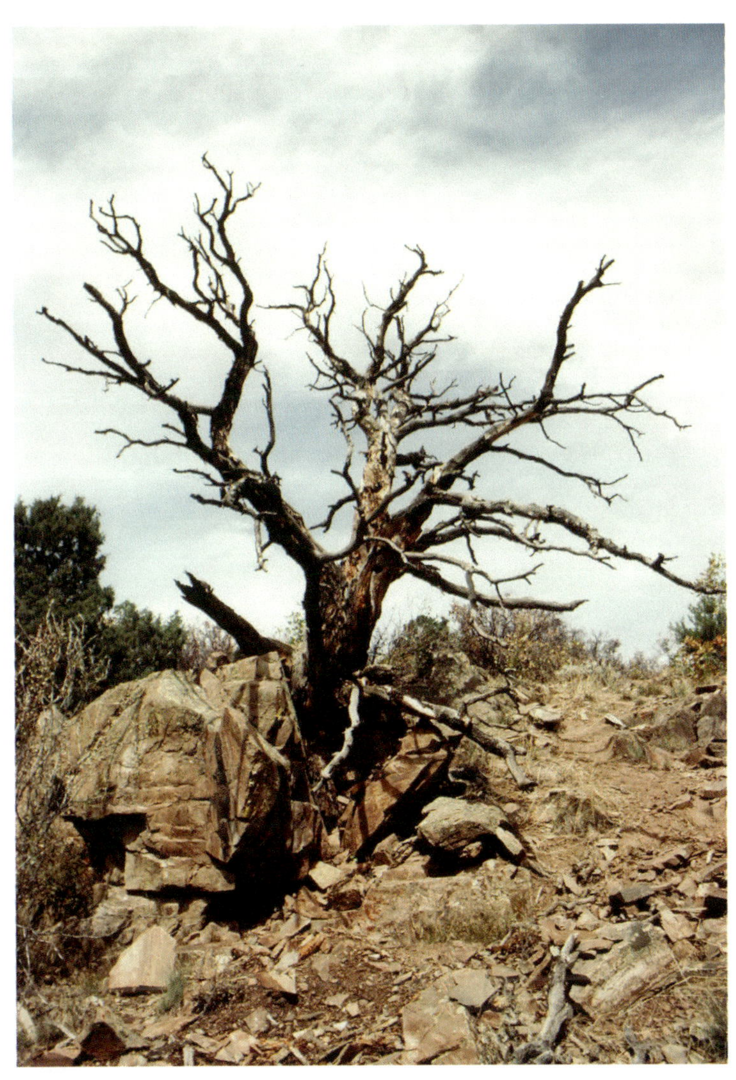

Kuma

Your father was anxious.
I remember his call:

Got your name
friend of a friend
said you're a photographer
might be interested
daughters are packing
Oregon to Florida
need a male
is it true you're a blackbelt
have a deal—car gas food film—
days would be yours—
roam take photos chase images—
at dusk
circle back
find their campsite
stay the night.

We both understood shadows—
how they are entities alive as the light.

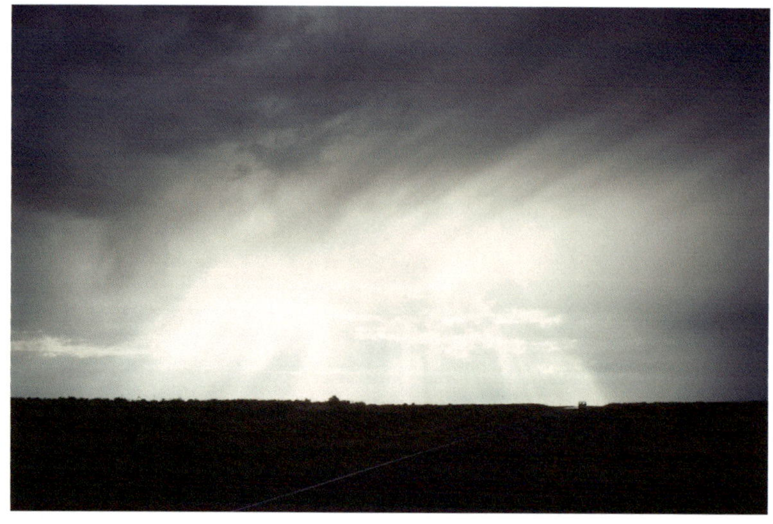

The Agreement

When he appeared at our door,
Ellen and I laughed—
our father had really found someone.

"Kuma quit his job, wants to be a photographer."
We didn't ask where he was from, his age,
or even if he liked to camp. Only the pact

concerned us. We led him to a table
where, like delegates sent to forge a deal,
we hovered over an open map.

Designating a beginning and end,
we inked routes across ten states,
signatures on a covenant.

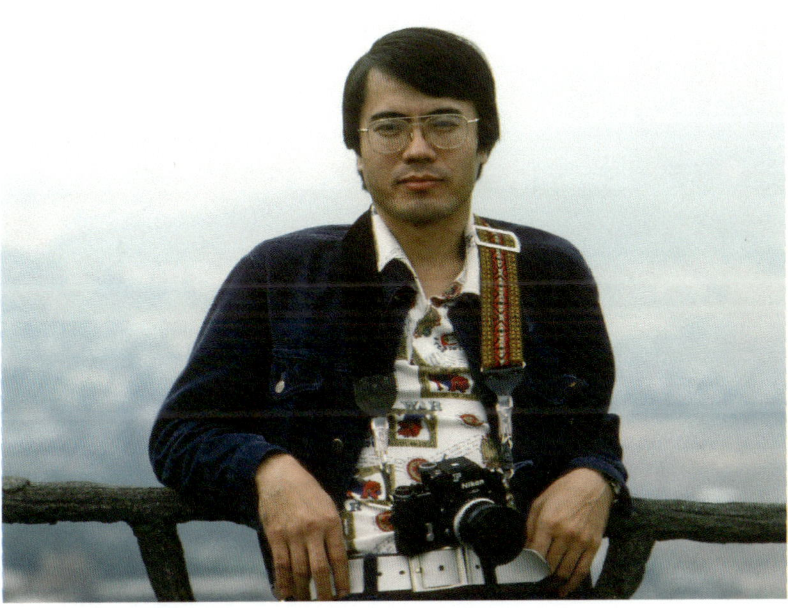

Seaside, Oregon

We'll dip our back tires in the Pacific ...

On the map, Seaside gleamed:
a carpet of sand, sun,
Ellen and I standing,
backs to the sea, bikes at our sides,
the shoreline beckoning.

Through the mist, Seaside emerged:
outcrops of black,
Ellen scrambling, cursing,
heaving her bike over wet rocks,
"Touch the water, let's go."

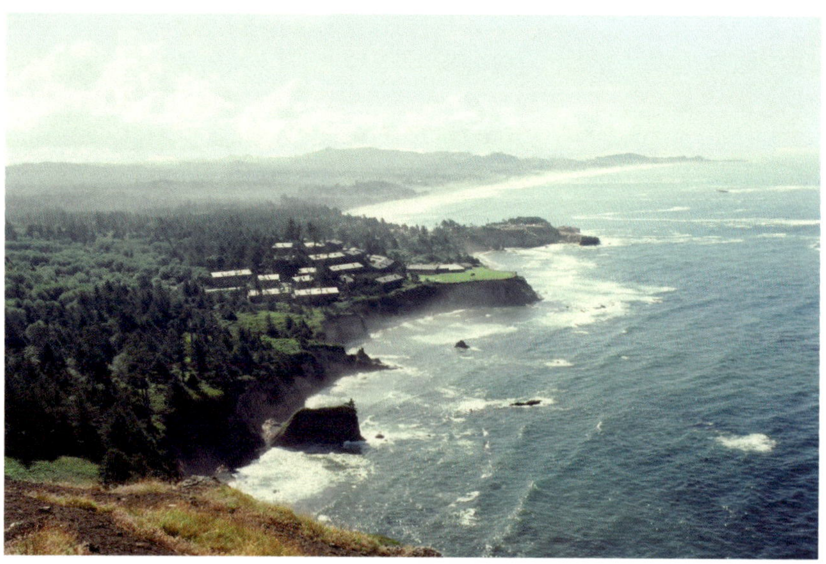

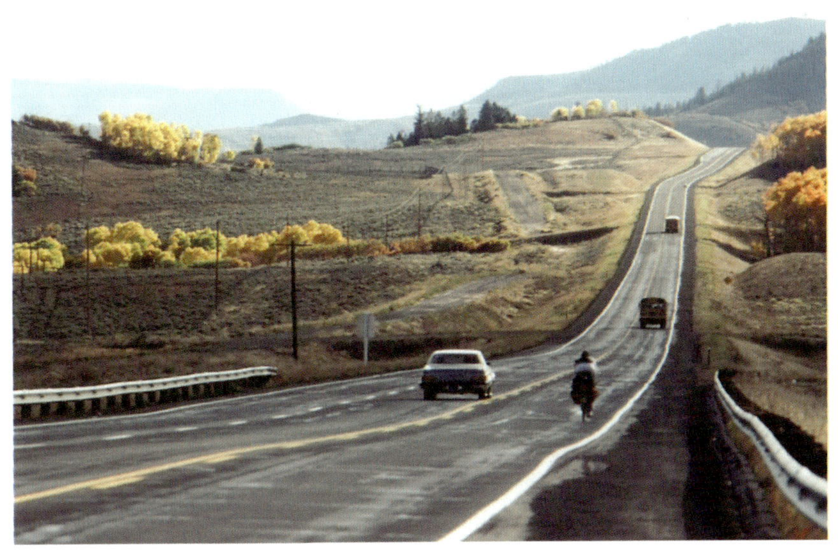

Tombstone Pass, Oregon

Between weather, terrain, mileage and route—

Should I be doing this? Will I get mail?
Who can I love? Who will love me back?

Litanies of self kept badgering
like the loggers passing, blasting their horns.
How tiresome their yelps.
Swerving as their flatbeds approached,
I imagined their lumber coming unhitched.

Sisters, Oregon

We stopped, laughed, leaned
our bikes against the sign.
What a confluence—city, sign, the two of us—
one layer aligned with another
like those transparencies in *The World Book*:
each sheet a view of the human body.
I used to love turning the pages,
placing the nervous system over the muscular,
the muscular over the circulatory,
veins in sync with tendons,
tendons with nerves. In front of the sign
we posed: photograph, genes, memory.
Even now as I write *sisters*, I feel coalescence
surging like a jolt of faith.

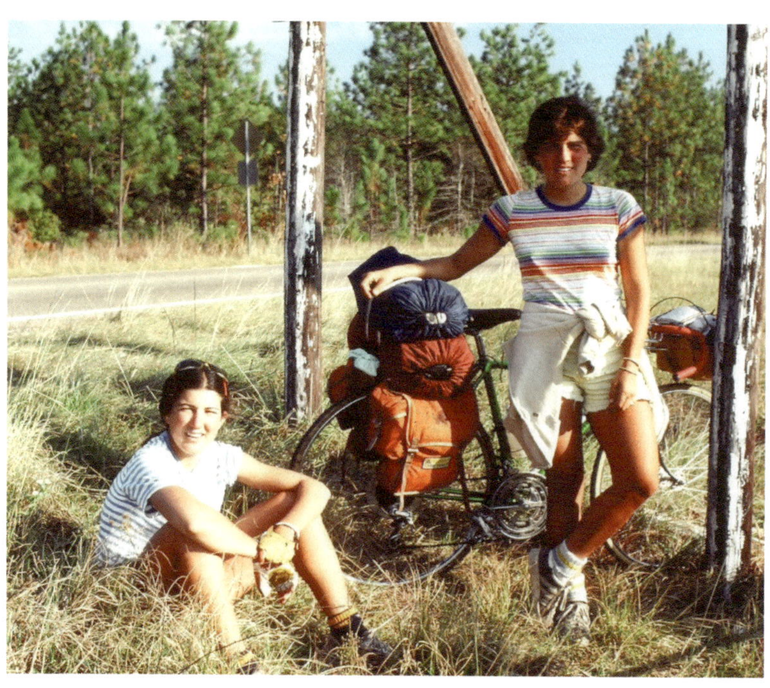

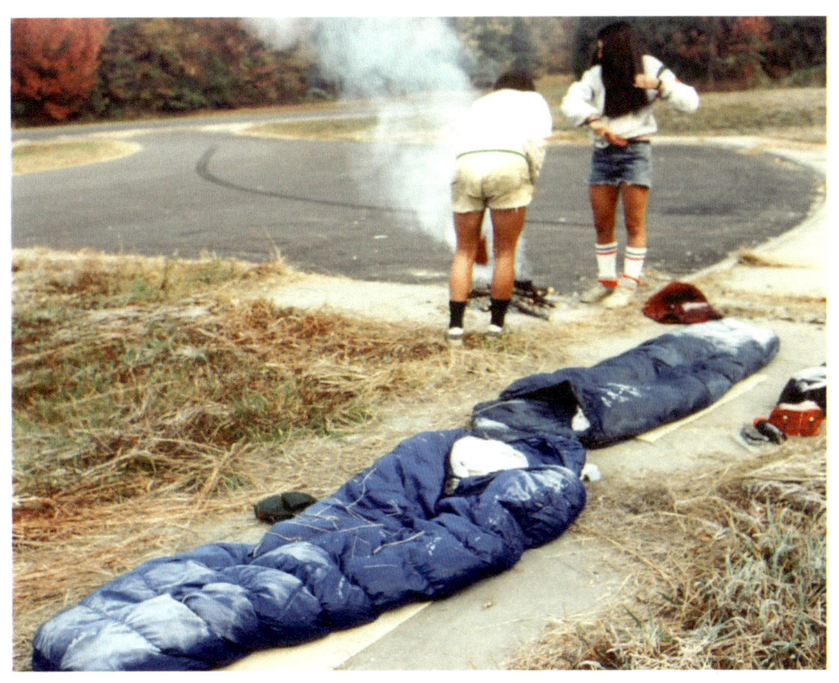

Murphy, Idaho

At first, I tried to dismiss the thump:
maybe it was the grade of the road.
But an untrue wheel nags,
rubs like an obsession.

Dropping my bike at the edge of a field,
I grabbed the rim, pushed and pulled, until,
without warning, the hub opened,
spilling forth tiny steel balls.

Nobody told me—
why didn't I know—
what were these orbs
strewn on the ground?

I stared at the silver moons,
this mini universe sealed inside,
and for a second I felt a rush
as if I were the first to discover a world.

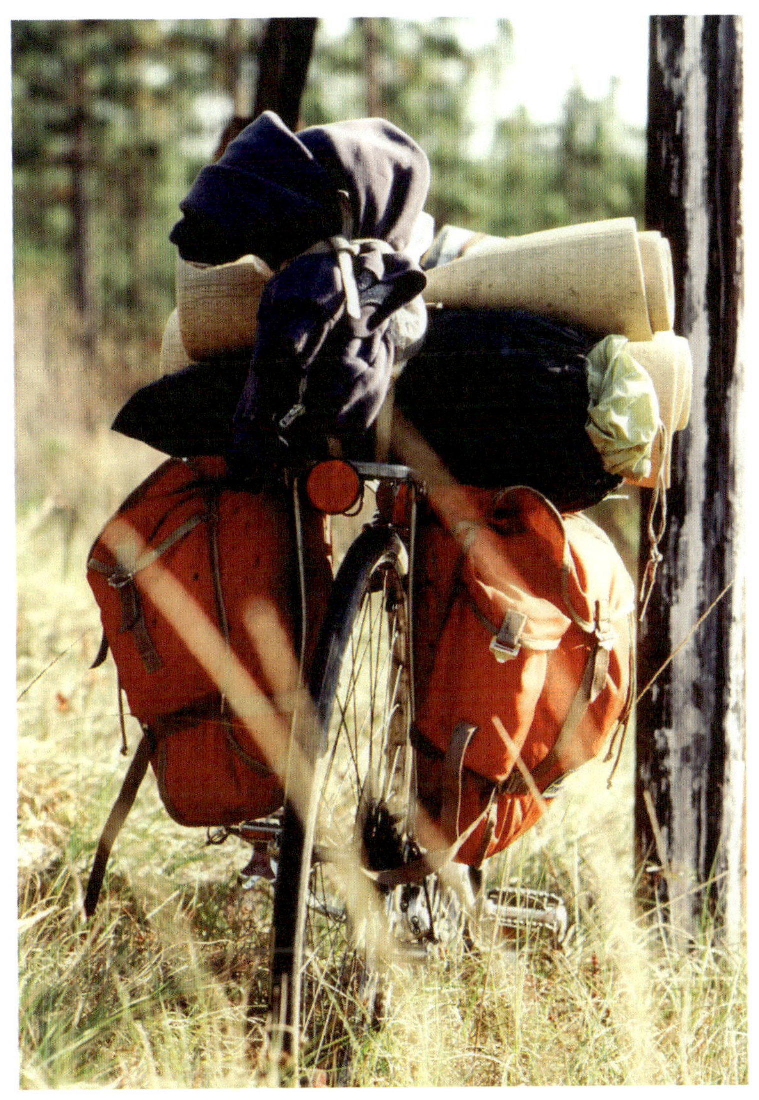

Breuno, Idaho

After dinner, as the campfire burned down,
Kuma would show us his moves.

Closing his eyes, he'd stand motionless
then, like a sprinter, explode.

We'd hear a snap, feel a gust.
Strength, he explained, lies coiled inside.

We took turns lunging and thrusting,
trying like him to splinter the air.

He let us practice. Jabbing and stabbing,
we pushed our fists at his bare chest.

He never moved—not when he absorbed
or let go. Were we that weak, was he that strong or

is stillness the pin that releases the spring?

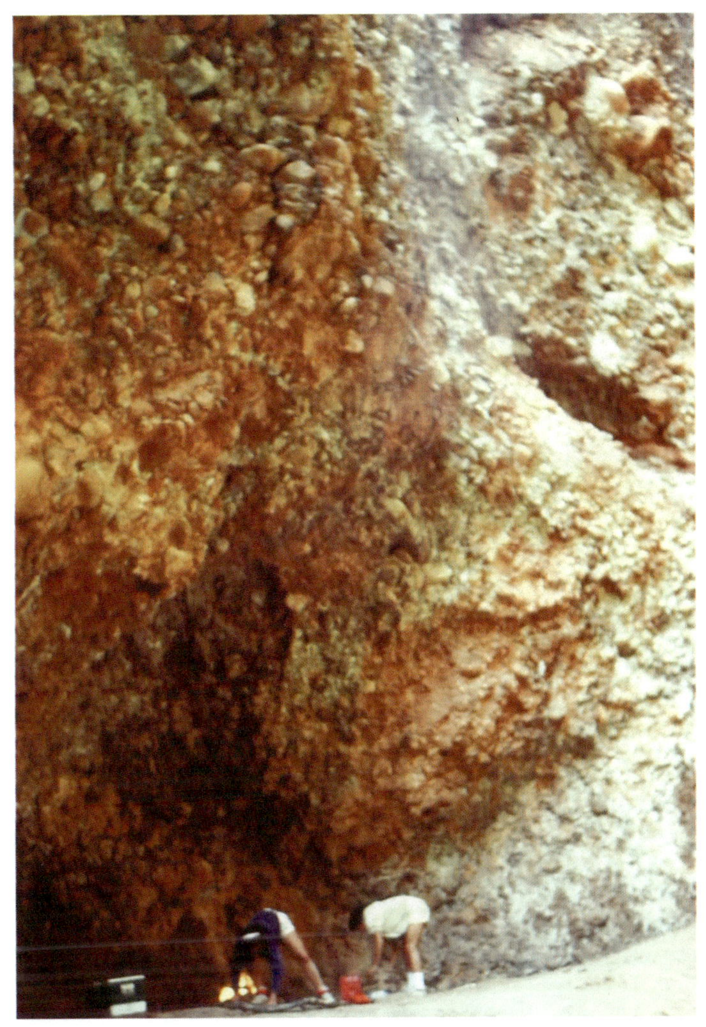

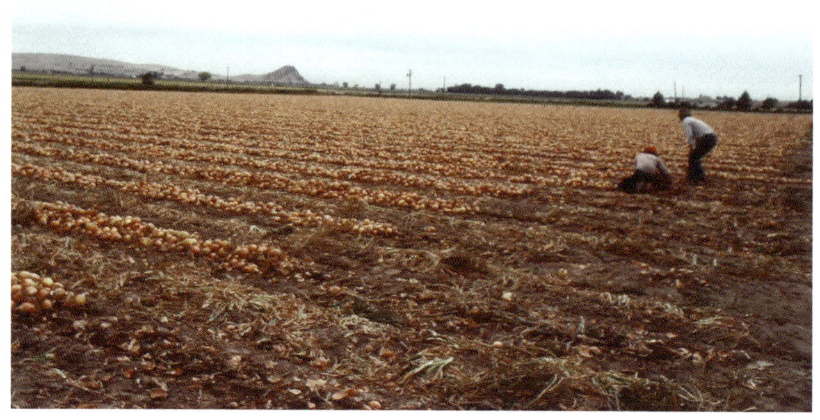

Hagerman, Idaho

When the migrant workers drove up to our site,
we froze. Finished for the day,
we unrolled our tent, began staking the floor.
They whistled, clicked their tongues.
We had passed them earlier,
seen their figures bent over a field,
admired the perfect Idaho scene.
But up close those figures were lurking men
and we were not cyclists untethered and free.
Grabbing our bikes, we rode up the hill.
Down below, our tent heaved then fell.

Provo, Utah

By chance we learned
if one of us rode in the other's wake
we could outwit the wind.
Along canyon rims, we traded leads—

I'd pedal ahead, lean in, count the minutes
when I could drop. In the eddy,
I'd close the gap, inch by inch,
edge up from behind, until I entered

that glorious calm.
A slit separated her tire from mine,
a margin so thin one careless brush
could topple us.

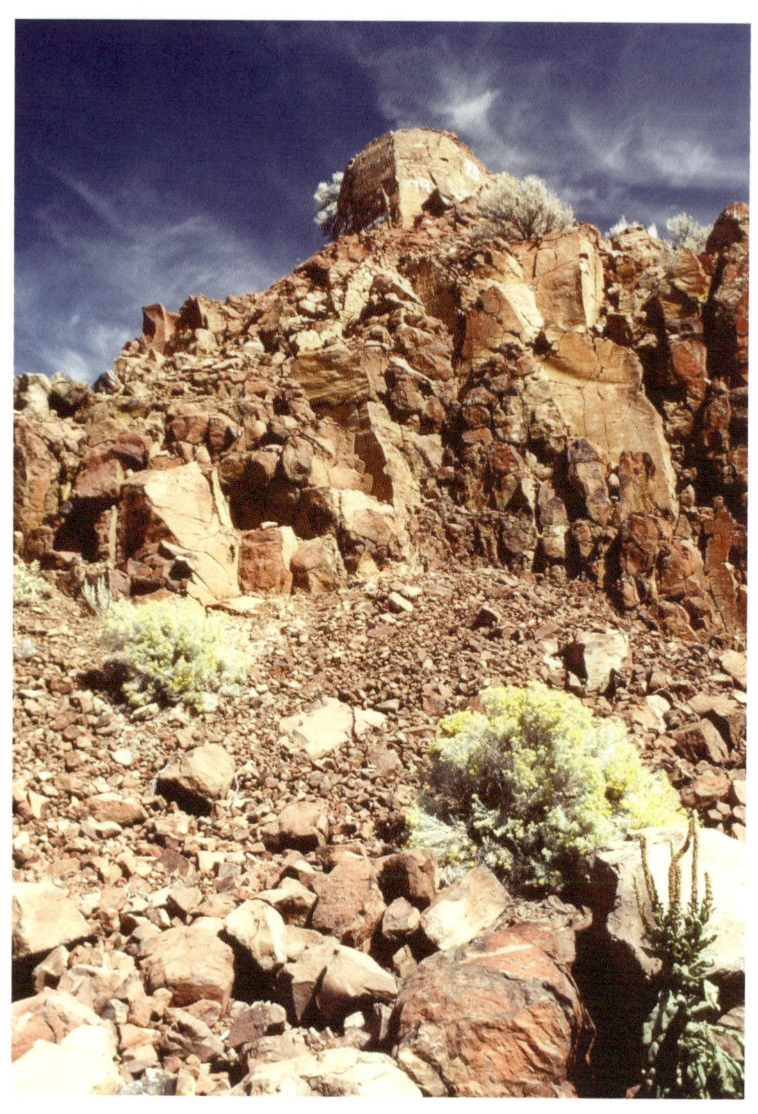

Green River, Utah

Every night we opened our map,
added up miles, circled the stop
we would cycle to next.
Time existed as a series of moves,
its passage marked by borders and towns.
Yesterday Thistle. Tomorrow Price.
We plotted ourselves like points on a graph,
measured 55 miles here to there.
By campfire, we charted our route,
studied terrain, our sacred text.

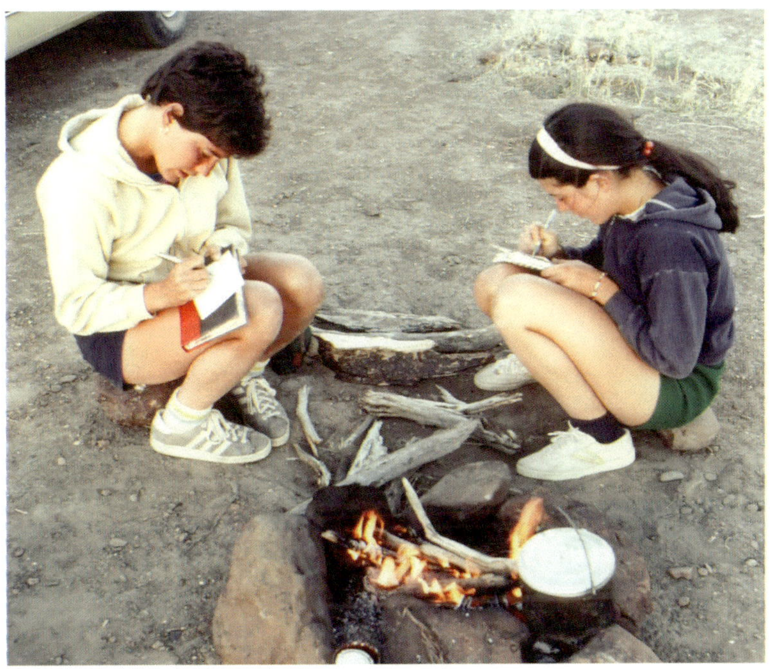

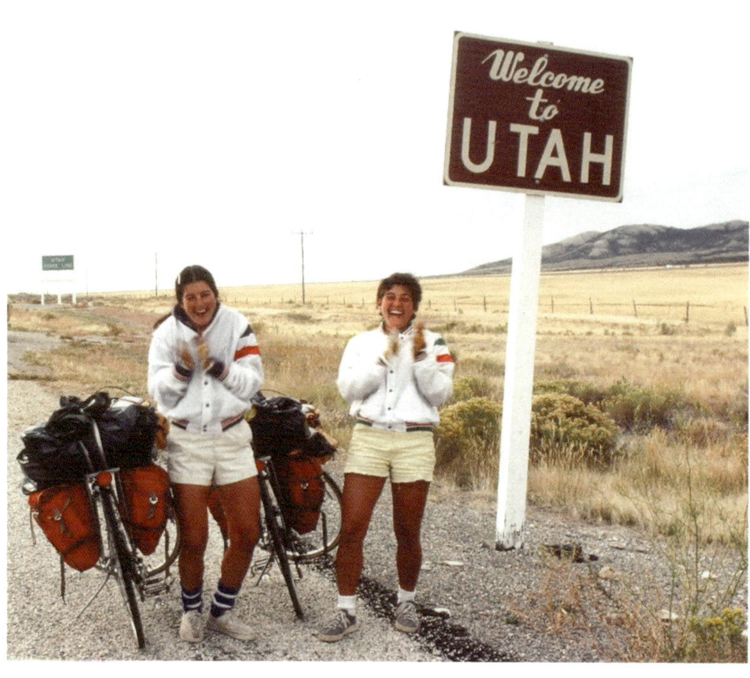
Welcome
to
UTAH

Montrose, Colorado

We feed the jukebox
while fretting over
Monarch Pass,
how high,
how far,
how long of climb,
rain, snow,
the road could close,
and switchbacks,
steep?
sharp?
pedal, walk?
Outside the diner,
we eye the peak,
head towards
its icy dare.

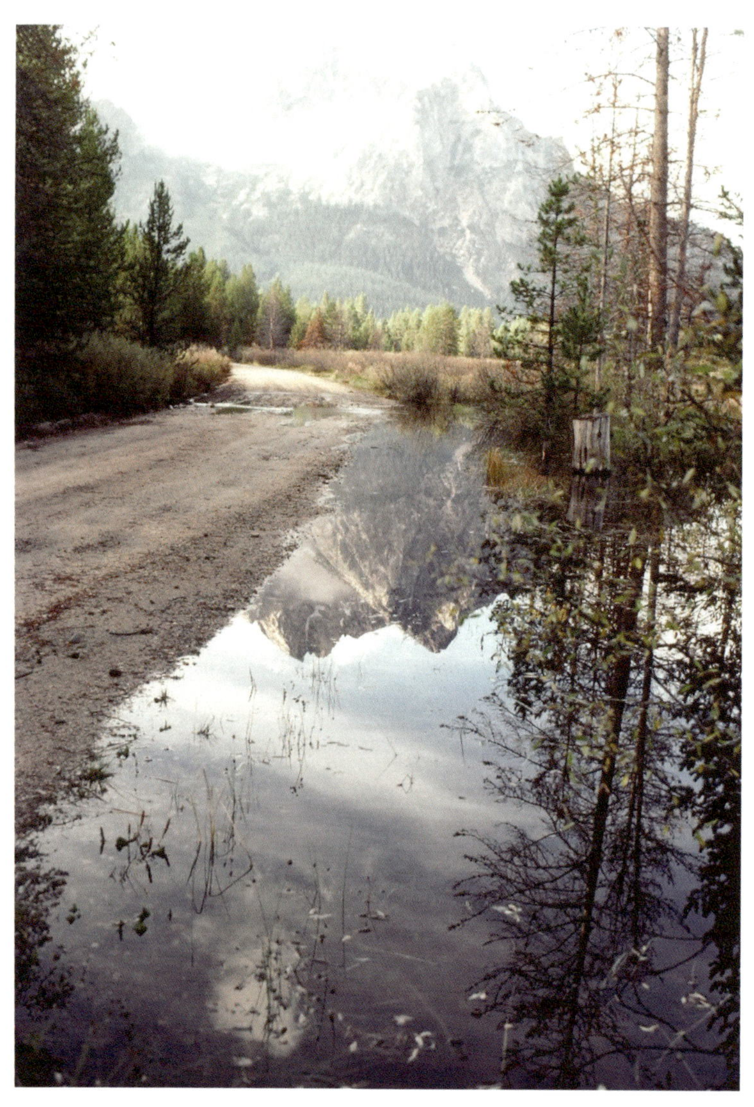

Monarch Pass, Colorado: Ascent

Oh Dream weaver
I believe you can get me through the night
Oh Dream weaver
I believe we can reach the morning light

– Gary Wright #2 on Billboard's Hot 100, 1976

yes
and up
up and up
I can go I can
I can make it oh
up and up make it
we can get up and up
past the night to the top
oh I can reach the light get
to the top yeah I can make it
there I believe we can pedal it
to the top can make my way up
ooooh Jane I believe I can make it
through the night fly high in the sky
on through the sleet can make it oooh
I can reach the morning light I can push
today's pain oooh dream weaver I believe
starry skies we can cross highways can push
make it through the night can fly so high to the
dream weaver I believe we can get there reach it
reach the top can make it through the night fly high
oooh Jane I believe we can reach the light all the way
to reach the light cross the highways forget the pain oh
Jane I believe you can make it through the night can push
can fly high through the starry skies forget today's rain ooh
we can make it through the night can reach the morning light
dream weaver I believe I can make it to the light dream weaver

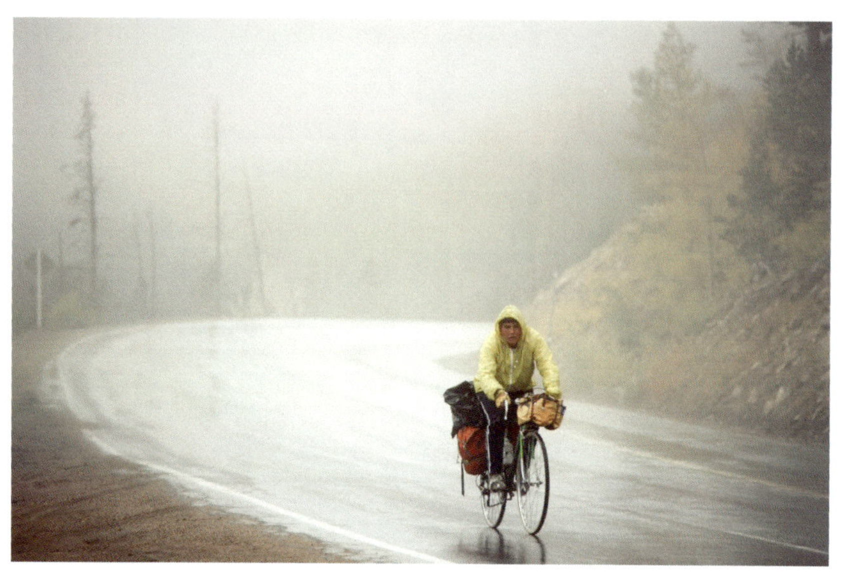

Monarch Pass, Colorado: The Crest

Elevation: 11,312 feet

Array of postcards—
snow-splashed pines, golden aspens—
we claim our summit.

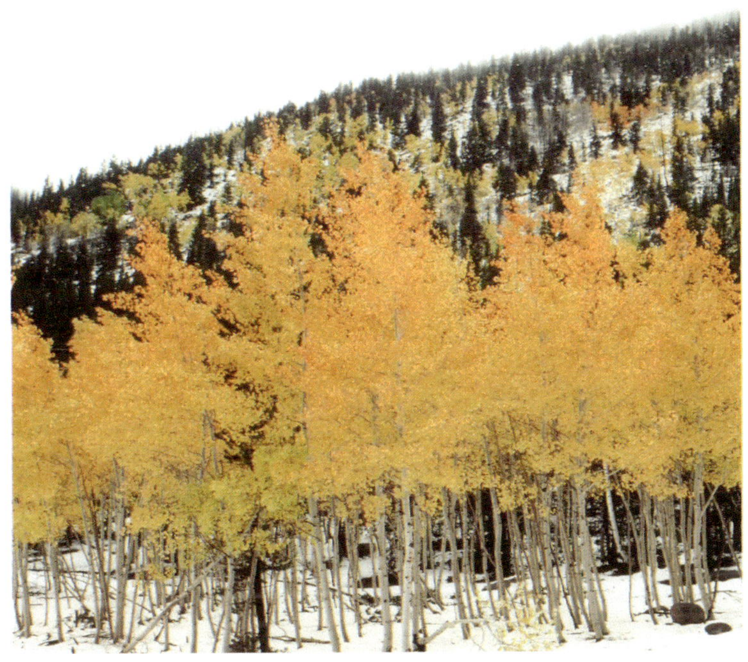

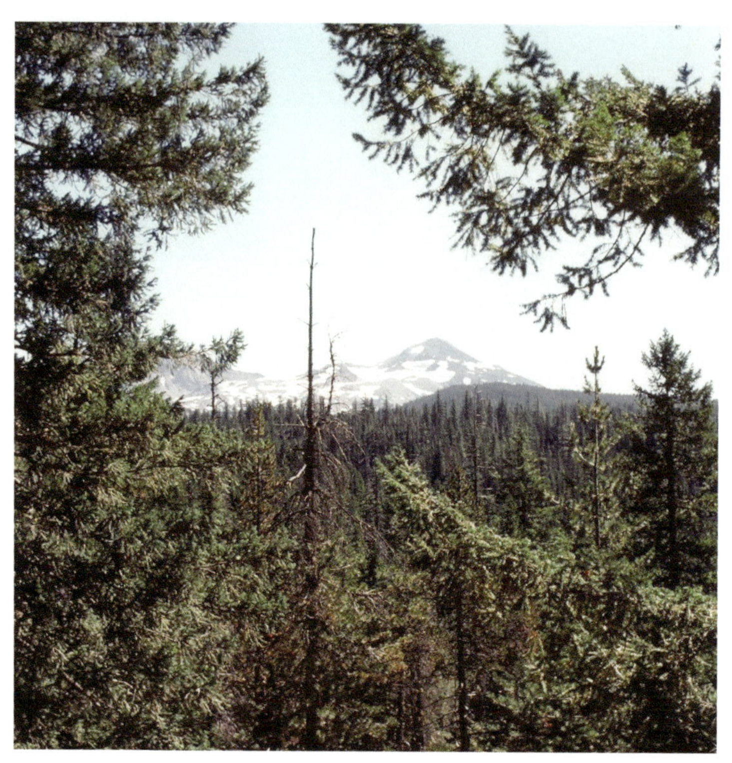

Monarch Pass, Colorado: Descent

Just when I stop
pumping my brakes
one hand on my handlebars
one fist in the air just when
I believe I can triumph over
any mountain
any moment
I control fate
this world
everything in it
just as I'm cruising
past the meadow
smiling
no fears
not a one

—whoosh—

I'm raised off the ground
my tires surging then
thrown down
a car
a voice
"You've been hit are you ok your bike..."

All I am thinking while brushing off dirt
there on the curb in the throes of the snarl
is how thrilling it felt
to be lifted up.

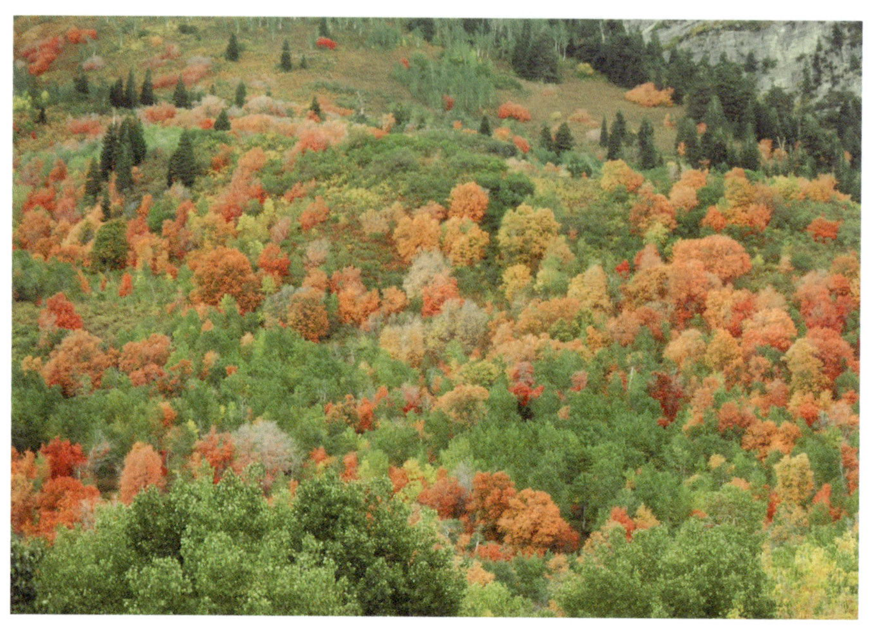

Boise City, Oklahoma

With flat roads and a tailwind
we were flying, crossing state lines
with sunlight to spare.
Nirvana, Flow, In the Zone.
Borders fused—
feet, pedals, rows of wheat.
Thoughts floated out of their ruts,
dispersed like milkweed.

So why did consciousness have to intrude,
snap its fingers, break the spell?
Like a town crier warning of doom, its karmic voice
swept in—*for every tailwind, a headwind*—
and just like that, bliss disappeared. Dread
returned as my amulet, a weapon to wave
like Kuma's nunchucks hidden
beneath his sleeping bag.

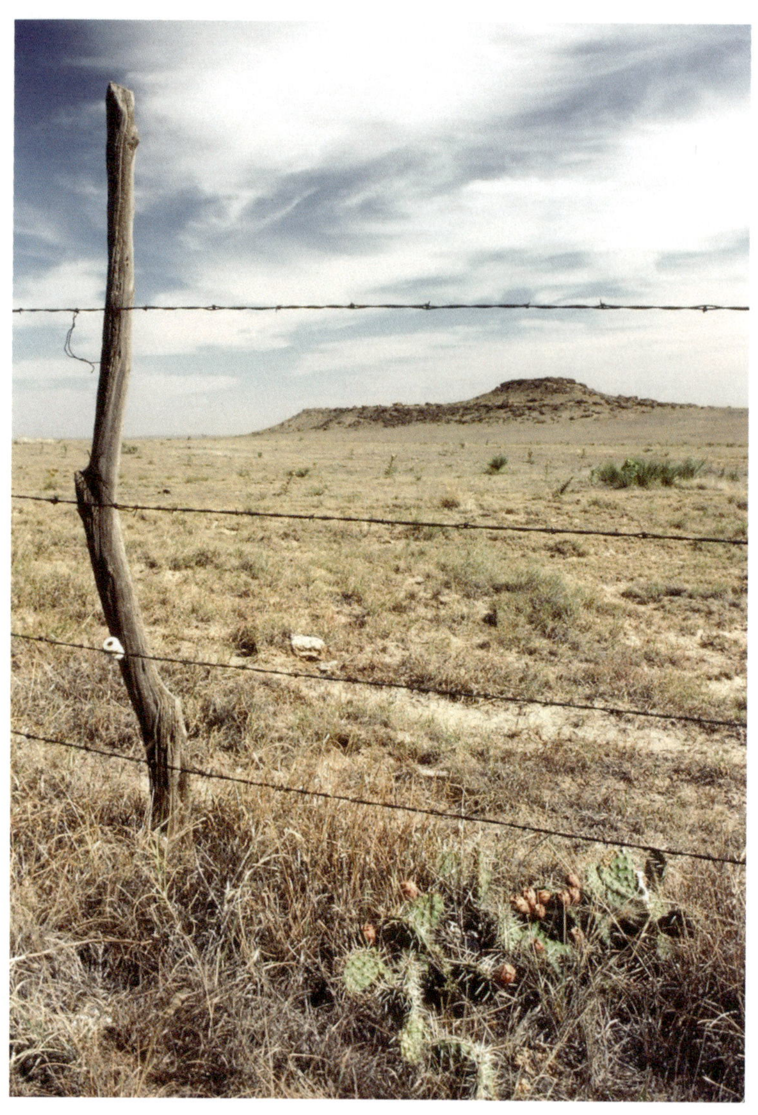

Electra, Texas

Frizzled and wind burnt, we take
to our tent long before the stars
come out. Once again no Kuma.
Every so often he vanishes.
Days pass before he appears,
smiling, waving across the road. He waits
for a perfect blend of image and light.

On my bike, I picture him
under a tree, sitting and sitting
like Buddha himself.
And I feel my own resolve pulsing
like a pumpjack in a Panhandle field,
up down, up down,
tapping the well.

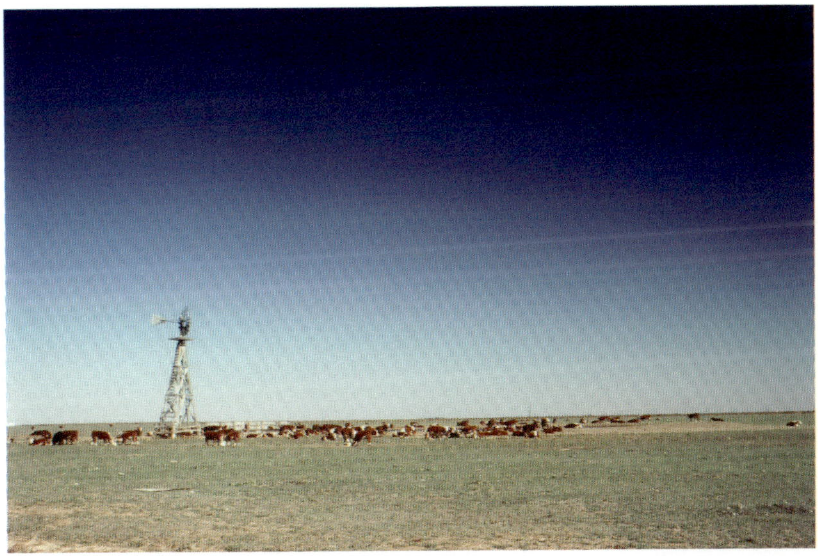

Farmersville, Texas

"Why do two young college girls set out on such a trip in the first place?"
The Farmersville Times, Oct. 25, 1976

hated school
needed escape

It's not as if I hadn't posed this question again and again, rehearsed my answer, but memory barged in, ransacked my thoughts:

broken heart
lonely

It took a few seconds to clear the debris:

"We've always done a lot of biking and this is something we wanted to do—we get to ride our bikes and see a lot of country at the same time."

"Have you encountered any other cross-country cyclists along the way?"

"In Oregon, a cyclist on his final mile."

I remember his eyes
like opaque pools of pain

"He seemed happy."

I watched the reporter write down my words.

Sir, what you have are puddles of truth as impermeable as oil.

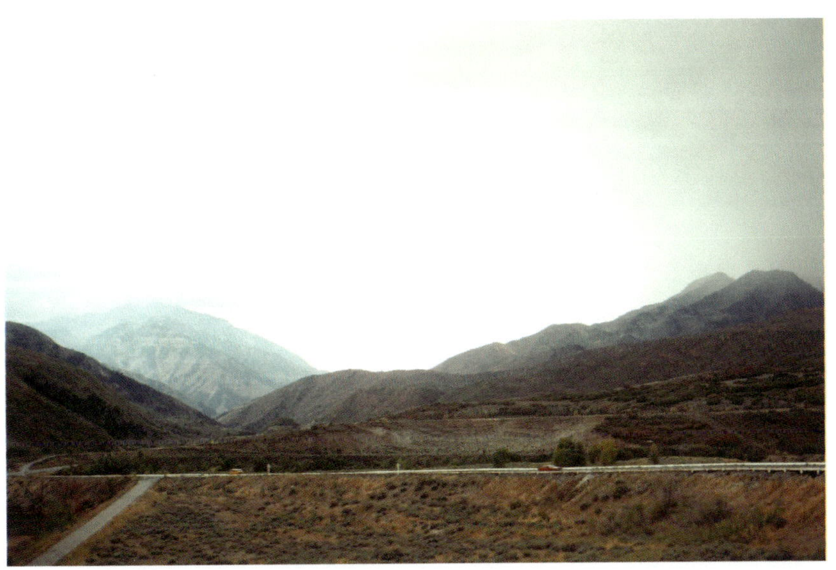

Denton, Texas

The wrangler saddled horses for us to ride
then dropped the reins and limped away,
no word of how or where, no hired guide,
no map, no trail, no one tracking our day.

Across a field, a meadow, along a county road,
into and out of a McDonald's drive-thru,
Ellen and I trotted horses and rode
up to a hilltop with a panoramic view.

Below lay a swath of motels and homes,
a Ponderosa sign blinking *All You Can Eat,*
pick-up trucks hauling gasoline drums,
smoke spewing from a meat-packing plant.

I knew as we lingered above the din
I would never feel this free again.

Grambling, Louisiana

Grocery stores, laundromats,
all-white towns, all-black.
Wherever we went, people stared.
At first we enjoyed their collective gaze—
we had never felt exotic before—
but after a while, their silence bored holes:
Is that surprise or disdain beneath their glare?
Self-doubt like water began to seep in:
Are we bold or reckless?
Voices resurfaced:
What for? Should I?
Why do two young college girls set out...
How quickly confidence breaks,
is patched,
breaks again
like potholes.

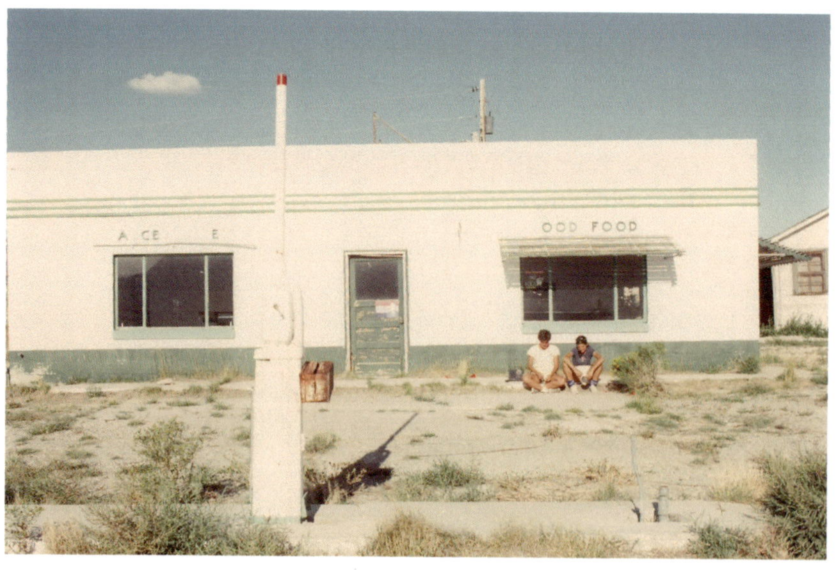

Tallulah, Louisiana

We were so happy in that motel room,
Kuma fresh from a shower,
Ellen and I knitting, the TV on.
It wasn't until the voice shook the pane,
barreled through like a spiraling wind,
that we opened the door.
"Get your ass out!"
What? Who? Why?
"Five minutes or I'll call the police!"
Is this the same man
who had welcomed us both, smiled
and joked as he gave us the key?
He's pointing at Kuma,
waving his fist
(but we told him we were expecting a third).
The police!
His glass eye is bulging.
Kuma's packing his bags,
scurrying around,
we are shaking
bewildered…
"Dumb ass gook!"
Suddenly
it all comes clear—
the heat, the energy,
what is driving this storm.
Our naïveté sank inside that eye.

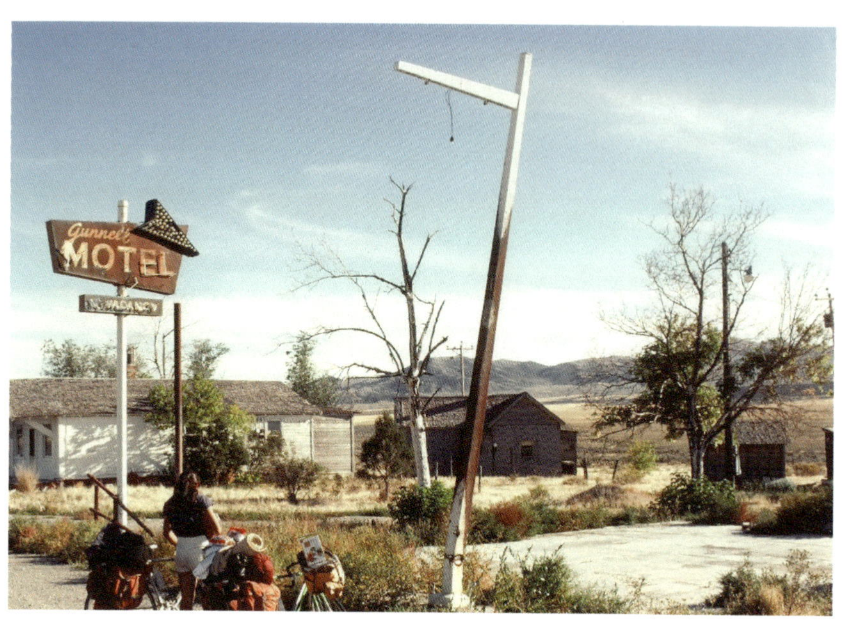
MOTEL

Vicksburg, Mississippi

With no shoulder to ride on we walked
our bikes across Vicksburg Bridge.

As trucks blasted past us hauling their freights,
we clung to the right of the solid white line.

Whatever you do, I reminded myself,
stay focused on the solid white line.

Steadily, we made our way like needles
stitching a fabric's seam. Eventually

I couldn't resist, couldn't stem the urge
to turn my head, glance over steel trusses

at the river below. Memory swelled, its muddy swirl
dragging my mind: every St. Louis summer

I'd hear of someone who went for a swim,
ignored warnings, dove right in,

(glancing, I felt a passing rig),
the body later washing on shore.

That's the danger of undertow,
also the thrill.

Magee, Mississippi

The sign read
Tattoos and Guns
so why did we
drop our bikes
ring the bell
step inside
what made us
linger amid
rifles and ink
let a man with a braid
and a bicep of skulls
pierce our skin
why did we trade
our parents' trust
for a daisy
(left hip for me right for you)
what were we thinking
as blood bubbled up
as we dabbed
paid
ran outside
laughing screaming
rode off abreast.

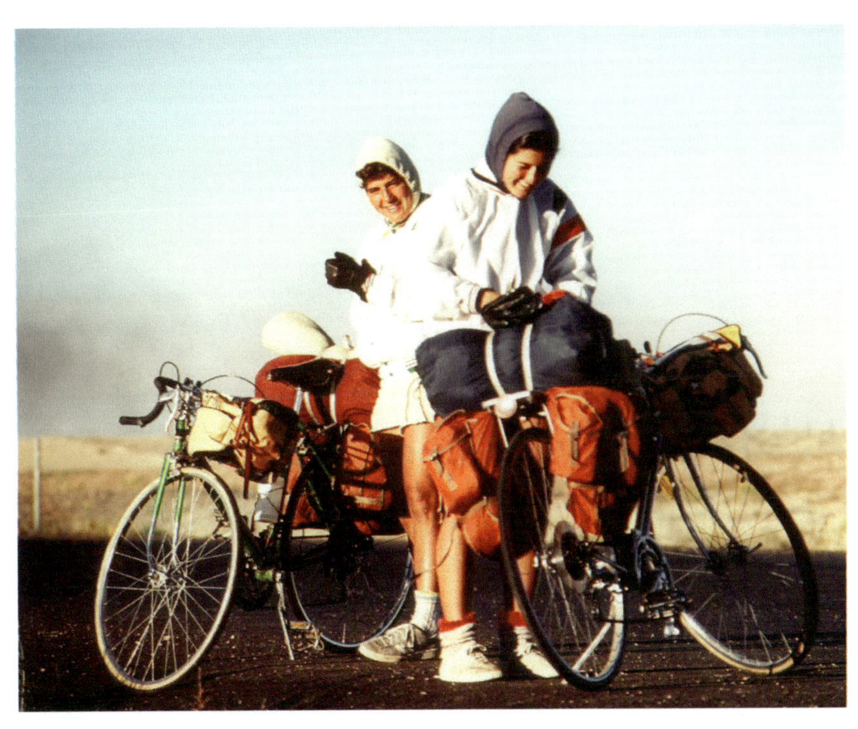

Wilmer, Alabama

What a welcome—palm tree
after palm tree waving at us.
Like teens at a concert
they danced and swayed, their fronds
clapping to an imagined beat.
I wanted to join the fun:
beach, hotel, lotion, sun.
But we still had two states,
and glee is unreliable
like the orange dates
littering roads,
brilliant but inedible.

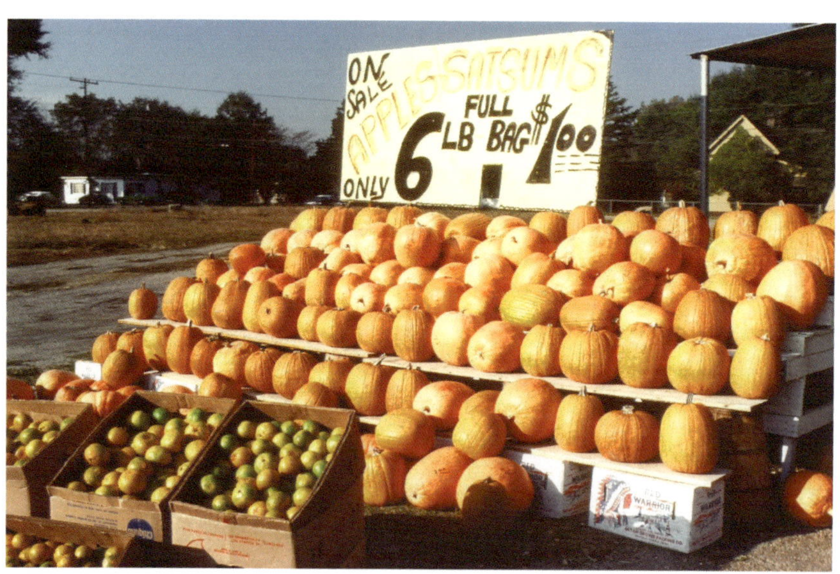

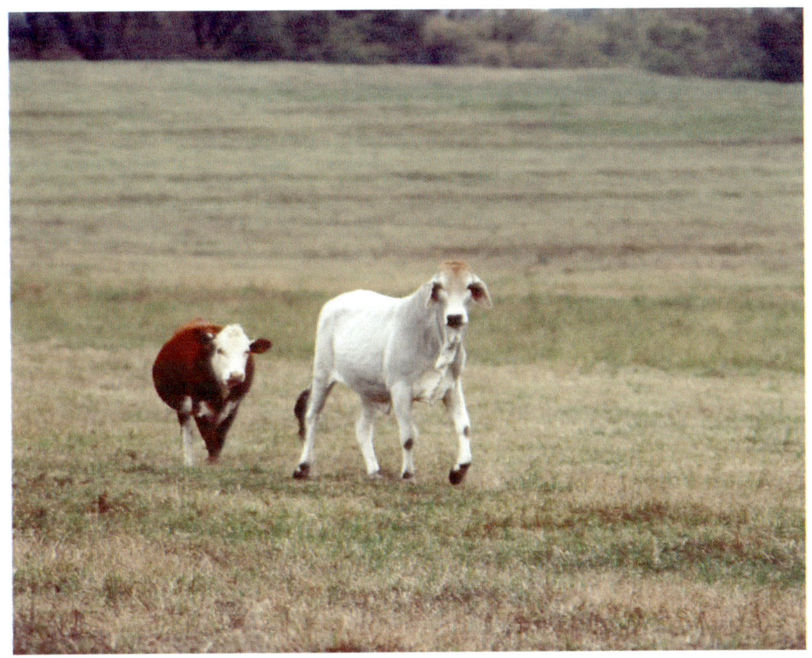

Loxley, Alabama

Because we asked for directions she invited us in, which is why
we found ourselves in a trailer on the black side of town, listening
to rules of dog racing. While her daughter served us sausage and eggs,
the woman held forth—"Quiniela," "Perfecta," "Trifecta." Each term
carried her back to the track, away from her kitchen where
a Japanese man and two white girls sat eating. *Take a look,*
I wanted to say, but the mother was dreaming:
"If it rains bet on the inside tracks." Her daughter was now
watching TV. Only the grandmother attended, off in the corner,
smiling at us with her toothless grin. *Everyone, take a look.*
What are the odds of our crossing?

Pensacola, Florida

We had no Circe to caution us,
no sailors to bind us to a mast.
When we saw the flash of a rising white cap,
we headed down the gravel path.
Like a southern mistress, the Gulf sashayed,
threw sprays of kisses,
whispered, winked:
I have all that she has,
salt, sand, the seagulls' caws.
Weathered and spent,
we unfolded our map
—from here to the sea 500 miles.
Couldn't we maybe just call it a day?
We hemmed and hawed
while the Gulf pressed on,
lulling us with her soothing cliché:
It's the journey not the finish,
as if this refrain could reel us in,
make us believe the means was the end.

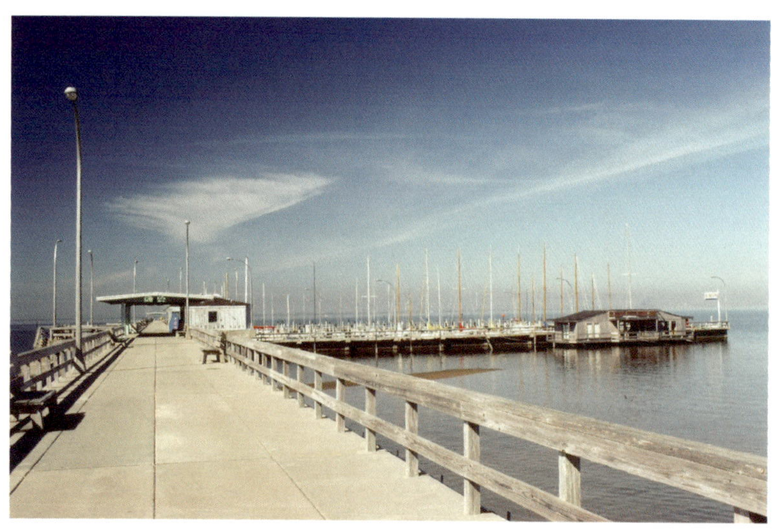

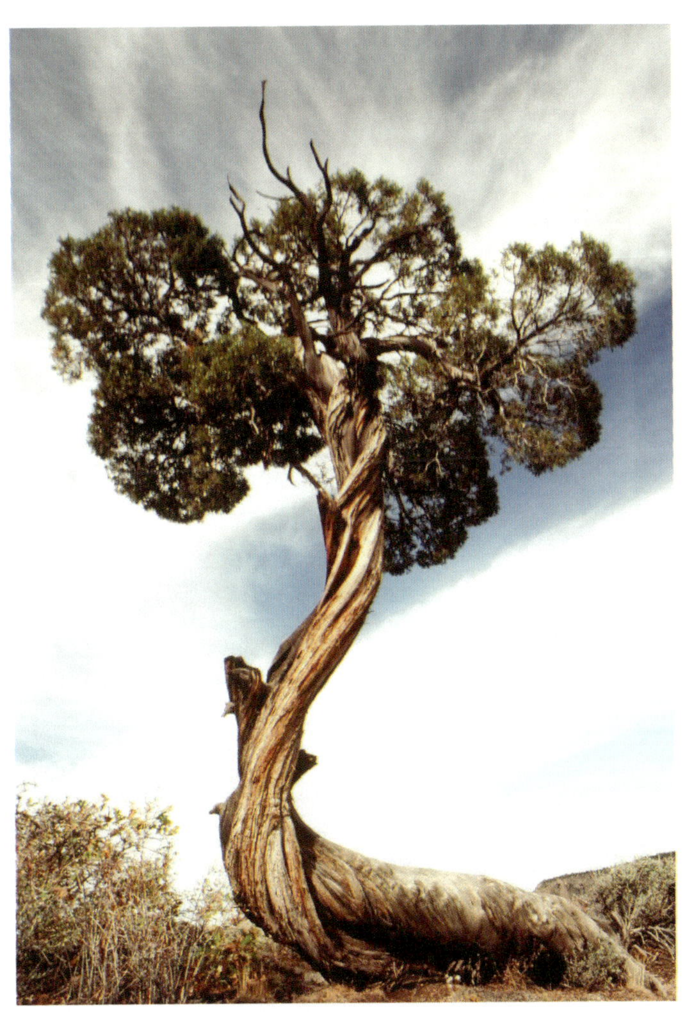

Father

Quit now?
The Gulf?
So close?
But why?
You're cold?
And wet?
Can't push?

Give all?
Regret?
The goal?
The dream?
No way.

Make it to the Atlantic!

Perry, Florida

Hat, gloves, sweatshirt, pants—
at every campground we left some gear.
Layer by layer, we shed our trip.
No need to restock spices and rice, WD 40.

Across the Panhandle we lightened our loads.
Cycling past forests and woods,
I daydreamed—beach, ocean, school, home—
wondered how I would reenter my life.

Just as I'd start to make a plan, bushwhack
to a future me, I'd hear hunters' shots
behind the pines, high-pitched squeals,
whelps echoing deep inside.

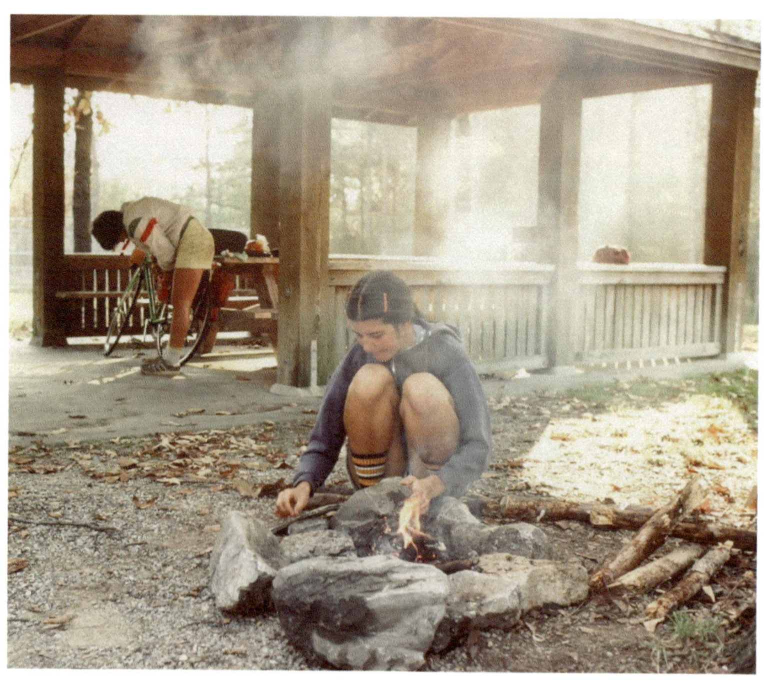

Crescent Beach, Florida

. . . and our front tires in the Atlantic

Why do two young college girls set out on such a trip in the first place?

Have you ever stood on the edge of a shore looked at the sea
absorbed in your worries thoughts
not really seeing the sea though your eyes are fixed on the water
but you're swimming in your own pool
feeling anxious bored thinking maybe you'll leave get a drink
when suddenly in the distance
you catch a glimmer of something you're not sure what
so you keep watching looking
really looking and then you see it and you're sure that glint
is a fin breaking through
rising vanishing rising and you can't take your eyes off the sea
you're staring ahead
so focused so absorbed in the water the air the creature
that you wait through
heat thirst restlessness for a flash of life entering light
blowing out spray
before it descends and you are grateful to be present
absorbed in that moment
when air sea fin merge in a synchronicity of wholeness
a moment of why.

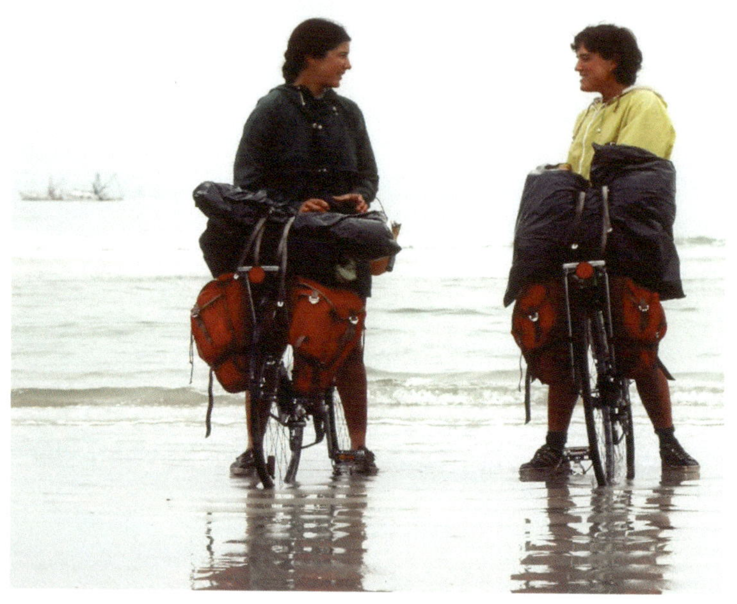

Sometimes in the morning

before opening my eyes,
I dream of our tent,
that tiny green dome.
From behind its walls
thin as skin, I hear birds,
leaves, a brush of wind.
I yearn for that waking,
that untethered dawn
when unzipping the door
I leaned into the world.

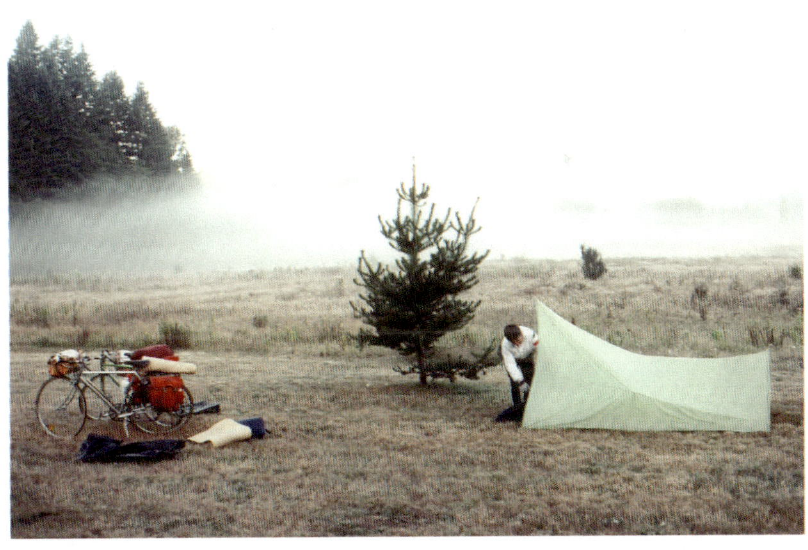

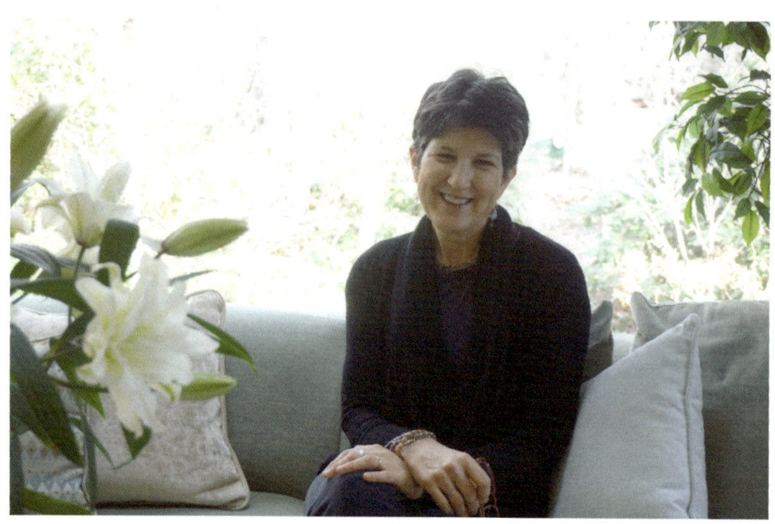

Jane Schapiro is the author of a volume of poetry, *Tapping This Stone* (Washington Writers' Publishing House, 1995) and the non-fiction book *Inside a Class Action: The Holocaust and the Swiss Banks* (University of Wisconsin, 2003), selected for the Notable Trials Library. Her chapbook *Mrs. Cave's House* won the 2012 Sow's Ear Poetry Chapbook competition. Her poems have appeared in publications such as *The American Scholar, Christian Science Monitor, The Gettysburg Review, Prairie Schooner, The Southern Review, The Sun, Women's Review of Books*, and *Yankee.* She is an academic tutor in the Athletic Department of George Mason University in Fairfax, Virginia. Her website is www.janeschapiro.com.

This book is set in Garamond Premier Pro, which had its genesis in 1988 when type-designer Robert Slimbach visited the Plantin-Moretus Museum in Antwerp, Belgium, to study its collection of Claude Garamond's metal punches and typefaces. During the mid-fifteen hundreds, Garamond—a Parisian punch-cutter—produced a refined array of book types that combined an unprecedented degree of balance and elegance, for centuries standing as the pinnacle of beauty and practicality in type-founding. Slimbach has created an entirely new interpretation based on Garamond's designs and on compatible italics cut by Robert Granjon, Garamond's contemporary.

To order additional copies of this book
or other Antrim House titles, contact the publisher at

Antrim House
21 Goodrich Rd., Simsbury, CT 06070
860.217.0023, AntrimHouse@comcast.net
or the house website (www.AntrimHouseBooks.com).

•

On the house website
in addition to information on books
you will find sample poems, upcoming events,
and a "seminar room" featuring supplemental biography,
notes, images, poems, reviews, and
writing suggestions.

CPSIA information can be obtained at www.ICGtesting.com
Printed in the USA
BVIW12n0002040417
480128BV00001B/1